Probability Skills Edexcel Maths Higher GCSE 9-1

Revision & Practice

GCSE 9-1

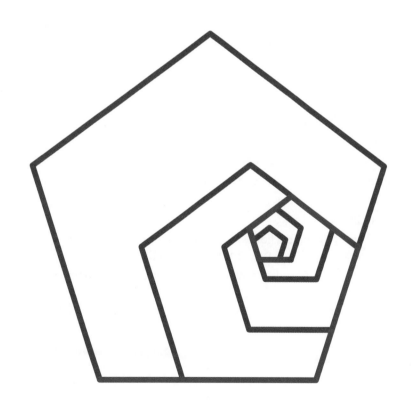

Build confidence with targeted skills practice

First published in the UK by Scholastic, 2017; this edition published 2024
Scholastic Distribution Centre, Bosworth Avenue, Tournament Fields, Warwick CV34 6UQ
Scholastic Ireland, 89E Lagan Road, Dublin Industrial Estate, Glasnevin, Dublin D11 HP5F

www.scholastic.co.uk

A CIP catalogue record for this book is available from the British Library.
ISBN 978-0702-33236-4
Printed by Leo Paper Products, China

The book is made of materials from well-managed,
FSC®-certified forests and other controlled sources.

Author Stephen Doyle
Editorial team Rachel Morgan, Audrey Stokes, Julia Roberts, Haremi Ltd
Series designers emc design ltd
Typesetting York Publishing Solutions Pvt. Ltd. & QBS Learning
Illustrations York Publishing Solutions Pvt. Ltd.
Cover illustration Golden Ratio, david.costa.art/Shutterstock

Notes from the publisher

Please use this product in conjunction with the official specification and sample assessment
materials. Ask your teacher if you are unsure where to find them.

The marks and star ratings have been suggested by our subject experts, but they are to be used as
a guide only.

Answer space has been provided, but you may need to use additional paper for your workings.

Contents

How to use this book

Inside this book you'll find everything you need to boost your skills in Probability to help you succeed in the GCSE 9–1 Edexcel Higher Mathematics specification. It combines revision and exam practice in one handy solution. Work through the revision material first or dip into the exam practice section as you complete each subtopic. This book will focus on probability but within your revision you will of course include other topics to ensure overall success. This book gives you the flexibility to revise your way!

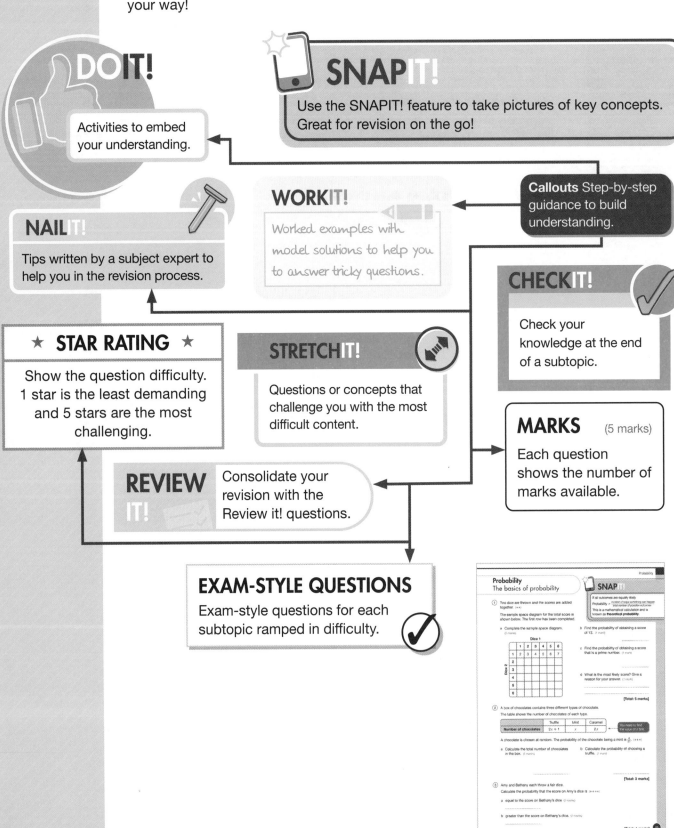

DO IT!

Activities to embed your understanding.

SNAP IT!

Use the SNAPIT! feature to take pictures of key concepts. Great for revision on the go!

Callouts Step-by-step guidance to build understanding.

WORK IT!

Worked examples with model solutions to help you to answer tricky questions.

NAIL IT!

Tips written by a subject expert to help you in the revision process.

CHECK IT!

Check your knowledge at the end of a subtopic.

★ STAR RATING ★

Show the question difficulty. 1 star is the least demanding and 5 stars are the most challenging.

STRETCH IT!

Questions or concepts that challenge you with the most difficult content.

MARKS (5 marks)

Each question shows the number of marks available.

REVIEW IT!

Consolidate your revision with the Review it! questions.

EXAM-STYLE QUESTIONS

Exam-style questions for each subtopic ramped in difficulty.

REVISION

The basics of probability

The probability scale

The probability scale goes from 0 to 1. Probabilities can be expressed as decimals or fractions.

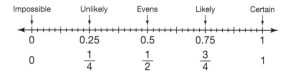

The probability formula

If all the outcomes are equally likely to happen:

$$\text{Probability} = \frac{\text{number of ways something can happen}}{\text{total number of possible outcomes}}$$

WORKIT!

Find the probability of throwing an even number on an unbiased dice.

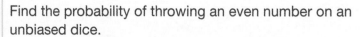

$$\text{Probability} = \frac{\text{number of ways something can happen}}{\text{total number of possible outcomes}} = \frac{3}{6} = \frac{1}{2}$$

Number of even numbers = 3 (2, 4 and 6).

Total number of numbers = 6.

Always cancel fractions, as otherwise you may lose marks.

The sum of probabilities

Suppose the probability that it rains tomorrow is $\frac{5}{8}$, then the probability that it does not rain tomorrow is $\frac{3}{8}$. When only one result can happen at a time the probabilities add up to 1:

$$\text{P(event occurs)} + \text{P(event does not occur)} = 1$$

If there are three possible probabilities, A, B and C, and only one can occur at once:

$$\text{P}(A) + \text{P}(B) + \text{P}(C) = 1$$

WORKIT!

A box contains coloured balls that are red, blue or green.

The table shows the number of balls of each colour.

	Red	Blue	Green
Number of balls	$2x + 1$	7	$x + 2$

A ball is chosen at random. The probability of the ball being blue is $\frac{7}{25}$.

Calculate the probability of choosing a red ball.

There are only red, blue and green balls in the bag, so the total probability must add up to 1.

$$P(blue) = \frac{number\ of\ blue\ balls}{total\ number\ of\ balls} = \frac{7}{25}$$

So total number of balls = 25

$2x + 1 + 7 + x + 2 = 25$ ← Add up the number of balls to create an equation.

$3x + 10 = 25$

$3x = 15$

$x = 5$

Number of red balls = $2x + 1 = 2 \times 5 + 1 = 11$ ← Use the calculated value of x to work out the number of red balls.

Probability of choosing a red ball = $\frac{11}{25}$

Sample space

In order to work out probability you need to be able to work out **outcomes**. The outcomes are the different possible combinations of what could happen. For example, when you toss two coins the possible outcomes are (HH, HT, TH and TT). You can use a **sample space** to show all the possible outcomes.

WORKIT!

A fair dice is rolled and a fair triangular spinner is spun. The scores are added together.

The outcomes are all the different ways of throwing the dice and spinning the spinner.

a Produce a sample space showing all the possible outcomes.

Spinner

		1	2	3
	1	2	3	4
	2	3	4	5
Dice	3	4	5	6
	4	5	6	7
	5	6	7	8
	6	7	8	9

The first column shows the score on the dice and the first row the score on the spinner.

The total scores are then filled in.

b Write down the total number of outcomes.

Total number of outcomes = 18 ← The number of outcomes is the number of totals in the sample space diagram.

c Find the probability of obtaining a total score of 7.

$$P(7) = \frac{number\ of\ ways\ of\ scoring\ 7}{total\ number\ of\ outcomes} = \frac{3}{18} = \frac{1}{6}$$

The dice and spinner are both fair, so all the outcomes are equally likely.

NAILIT!

An event is an outcome or group of outcomes you are interested in, such as 'it rains tomorrow' or 'it rains on Saturday and is fine on Sunday'.

You can work out the total number of outcomes using the formula:

Total number of outcomes = number of ways each action can be carried out, multiplied together

For the example above, total number of outcomes = number of dice outcomes × number of spinner outcomes: 6 × 3 = 18.

WORKIT!

A restaurant has a fixed price menu offering a choice of 4 starters, 6 mains and 5 desserts.

a How many different meals are possible? Assume that all the meals consist of one starter, one main and one dessert.

Total number of meals = 4 × 6 × 5 = 120

b What is the probability of choosing the first item on each of the starters, mains and desserts menus?

P(1st starter, 1st main, 1st dessert) = $\frac{1}{120}$

> Each outcome (combination of starter, main and dessert) is equally likely.

WORKIT!

Four fair dice are rolled.

a Calculate the number of possible outcomes.

Total number of outcomes = number of ways each action can be carried out, multiplied together

= 6 × 6 × 6 × 6 = 1296

b Calculate the number of possible ways of all the dice showing prime numbers.

> The possible prime numbers are 2, 3 and 5.

Number of prime numbers on 1 dice = 3

Number of possible outcomes for all prime numbers = 3 × 3 × 3 × 3 = 81

c Calculate the probability of all the dice showing prime numbers.

Probability of all prime numbers = $\frac{81}{1296}$ = $\frac{1}{16}$

DOIT!

Two coins are tossed. Work out the probability of one coin landing heads and the other landing tails.

✓ CHECKIT!

1 A five-sided spinner is spun 3 times. Find the probability of the spinner showing an even number every time.

2 There are 20 counters in a bag. 4 are black, 7 are red and 9 are green. One counter is picked at random from the bag.

a Write down the probability of obtaining a white counter.

b Calculate the probability that the counter picked is black, giving your answer as a fraction in its simplest form.

c Calculate the probability that the counter picked is **not** green.

Probability experiments

A probability experiment is an experiment, trial or observation that can be repeated numerous times under the same conditions. Each outcome of a probability experiment must not be affected by any other outcome and cannot be predicted with certainty.

Examples of probability experiments include:

- tossing a coin: two possible outcomes, heads or tails

- rolling a six-sided dice: six possible outcomes, the numbers 1 to 6

- selecting a numbered ball (1–50) from a bag: 50 possible outcomes.

Relative frequency

Relative frequency is an estimate of probability. For example, suppose you rolled a fair (i.e. unbiased) dice 500 times and recorded your results.

$$\text{Relative frequency} = \frac{\text{frequency of event}}{\text{total frequency}}$$

Total frequency (see table) = $91 + 77 + 99 + 74 + 93 + 66 = 500$.

The relative frequency for a score of $3 = \frac{99}{500} = 0.198$.

The relative frequencies can be used to create a table similar to the results table.

Score	Frequency
1	91
2	77
3	99
4	74
5	93
6	66

Score	1	2	3	4	5	6
Relative frequency	$\frac{91}{500} = 0.182$	$\frac{77}{500} = 0.154$	$\frac{99}{500} = 0.198$	$\frac{74}{500} = 0.148$	$\frac{93}{500} = 0.186$	$\frac{66}{500} = 0.132$

Relative frequency and probability

The relative frequency can be used to give an estimate of the probability.

The theoretical probability of a particular score on an unbiased dice = $\frac{1}{6}$ or 0.1666... as a decimal.

The relative frequencies are different from this value.

The more times the experiment is conducted, the closer the relative frequencies will be to the theoretical probability $\left(\frac{1}{6} \text{ in this case}\right)$.

> Note that all these relative frequencies add up to 1.

> The relative frequency will approach the theoretical frequency only over a very large number of trials.

WORKIT!

A five-sided spinner with sides numbered from 1 to 5 has the following relative frequencies of scores.

Score	1	2	3	4	5
Relative	x	0.05	$2x$	0.15	0.20

Calculate the value of x.

$$x + 0.05 + 2x + 0.15 + 0.20 = 1$$
$$3x + 0.4 = 1$$
$$3x = 0.6$$
$$x = 0.2$$

The total relative frequencies have to add up to 1.

Expected frequency

To work out an estimate of the number of times an event occurs (**expected frequency**) we can use the following formula:

Expected frequency = probability of the event × number of events

WORKIT!

A seed picked at random from a large batch of seeds has a probability of growing into a plant with yellow flowers of 0.12.

There are 200 seeds in a packet. Work out an estimate for how many seeds will grow into plants with yellow flowers.

Expected number of yellow plants = probability of yellow plant
× number of seeds
= 0.12 × 200
= 24

CHECKIT!

1 A six-sided spinner with numbers from 1 to 6 was spun 120 times. The results are shown in the table.

Number on spinner	1	2	3	4	5	6
Frequency	18	20	25	21	19	17

a Work out the relative frequency for a score of 3, giving your answer as a decimal to 2 decimal places.

b Work out the relative frequency for a score of 6, giving your answer as a decimal to 2 decimal places.

c Sean says that the answers to parts a and b should be the same so the spinner is not fair (i.e. it is biased). Is Sean right? Explain your answer.

2 A machine fills cans with 330 ml of cola. Out of a batch of 500 cans, 20 of them contained less than 330 ml of cola.

a Estimate the probability that the next can filled by the machine contains less than 330 ml of cola.

b The machine fills 15 000 cans per day. Estimate how many would contain less than 330 ml of cola.

3 In a batch of apples it was found that the probability of an apple being bad was $\frac{3}{40}$.

In a similar batch of 600 apples, how many would be expected to be bad?

The AND and OR rules

If events *A* and *B* are **mutually exclusive**, it means that event *A* can happen or event *B* can happen but they cannot both happen at the same time. When an event has no effect on another event, they are said to be **independent events**.

NAILIT!

Note the difference between independent events and mutually exclusive events.

There are two important laws that need to be remembered when working out probabilities. They are the **addition rule** and the **multiplication rule**. The addition rule is sometimes called the **OR rule** and the multiplication law is sometimes called the **AND rule**.

SNAPIT!   AND and OR rules

You must learn these formulae.

Probability of *A* or *B* happening: $P(A \text{ OR } B) = P(A) + P(B)$ ◄─── This formula only applies to mutually exclusive events.

Probability of *A* and *B* happening: $P(A \text{ AND } B) = P(A) \times P(B)$ ◄─── This formula only applies to independent events.

WORKIT!

1 A bag contains 3 red balls and 7 black balls. Ahmed picks one at random and notes the colour. He puts it back into the bag and picks another ball at random.

What is the probability that both balls are red?

$P(\text{1st red}) = \frac{3}{10}$ and $P(\text{2nd red}) = \frac{3}{10}$

$P(\text{red AND red}) = P(\text{1st red}) \times P(\text{2nd red}) = \frac{3}{10} \times \frac{3}{10} = \frac{9}{100}$ ◄─── The two events (picking each ball) are independent, as the balls in the bag are the same for each pick.

2   A computer manufacturer submits bids for three projects, A, B and C.

The probabilities of getting the order for projects A, B and C are $\frac{2}{5}$, $\frac{1}{3}$ and $\frac{1}{4}$, respectively. The probability of getting the order for each project is independent of the other projects.

Calculate the probability of the following events, making your methods clear. Give each answer as a fraction in its simplest form.

a The company gets all three orders.

$P(A \text{ and } B \text{ and } C) = \frac{2}{5} \times \frac{1}{3} \times \frac{1}{4} = \frac{1}{30}$ ← Use the AND rule.

b The company gets exactly one order.

A	Not B	Not C	$\frac{2}{5} \times \frac{2}{3} \times \frac{3}{4} = \frac{12}{60}$
Not A	B	Not C	$\frac{3}{5} \times \frac{1}{3} \times \frac{3}{4} = \frac{9}{60}$
Not A	Not B	C	$\frac{3}{5} \times \frac{2}{3} \times \frac{1}{4} = \frac{6}{60}$

$P(\text{exactly one order}) = \frac{12}{60} + \frac{9}{60} + \frac{6}{60} = \frac{27}{60} = \frac{9}{20}$

Make a table showing the possible outcomes for winning exactly one project.
P(not getting an order) = 1 − P(getting an order)
Use the AND rule to work out the probability of each of these outcomes.

DOIT!

Make a revision poster for the AND rule and the OR rule, including the necessary conditions.

✓ CHECKIT!

1   James passes two sets of traffic lights on his way to work. The probability he is stopped by the first set of traffic lights is 0.2 and the probability he is stopped by the second set of lights is 0.3. The two sets of traffic lights are independent.

   a Explain in relation to this question what independent events are.

   b Work out the probability that James is stopped by both sets of lights.

   c Work out the probability that James is not stopped by either set of lights.

2   The probability that Nala takes a packed lunch to school is $\frac{1}{4}$.

The probability that Nala cycles to school is $\frac{2}{3}$.

The probability that Nala has remembered her homework is $\frac{7}{8}$.

   a Work out the probability all of these events take place.

   b Work out the probability that none of the events takes place.

Tree diagrams

The probabilities of two or more events can be shown on a **tree diagram**.

Independent events

> The two events (picking the balls out) are independent because the first ball is put back into the bag.

WORKIT!

A bag contains 5 red and 4 blue balls. A ball is picked at random from the bag, the colour is noted and the ball is put back into the bag. Another ball is picked at random and its colour noted.

a Draw a tree diagram to show these events.

b Work out the probability that both balls are red.

$$P(\text{red and red}) = \frac{5}{9} \times \frac{5}{9} = \frac{25}{81}$$

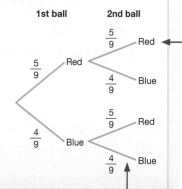

c Work out the probability that the balls are of different colours.

$$P(\text{red then blue}) = \frac{5}{9} \times \frac{4}{9} = \frac{20}{81}$$

$$P(\text{blue then red}) = \frac{4}{9} \times \frac{5}{9} = \frac{20}{81}$$

$$P(\text{different colours}) = \frac{20}{81} + \frac{20}{81} = \frac{40}{81}$$

> Because you can have either of these, use the OR rule.

> As the balls are replaced, the probability for the second ball is the same as for the first ball. The probabilities at each branch add up to 1 as you are certain to pick either a red or a blue ball.

Dependent events

In **dependent** events, one event influences another. This tree diagram shows the same problem as above, except that this time the first ball is **not** replaced. The probability for the second ball depends on what colour was picked for the first ball.

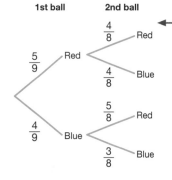

NAIL IT!

It is important to note that taking two things out without replacement is like taking one out without replacement and then taking the other out.

NAILIT!

Don't cancel fractions until the end of your answer. Adding the fractions is easier if they all have the same denominator.

> To work out the probability for a particular combination (e.g. a red and a red), multiply the probabilities on the two branches.

NAILIT!

Another way to do part c would be to find the probability that the colours of the balls are the same and then subtract this from 1.

> If a red ball is picked and not replaced, there are only 4 red balls and 8 balls in total for the second pick.

WORKIT!

The probability that it rains on Monday is 0.3.

If it rained on Monday, the probability of it not raining on Tuesday is 0.4.

If it did not rain on Monday, the probability of it not raining on Tuesday is 0.6.

a Draw a probability tree diagram showing this information.

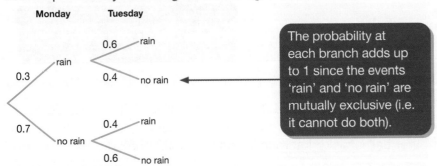

The probability at each branch adds up to 1 since the events 'rain' and 'no rain' are mutually exclusive (i.e. it cannot do both).

b It rained on only one of the two days. Is it more likely that it rained on Monday or Tuesday? Show your working.

P(only rained on Monday) = P(rain Monday) × P(no rain Tuesday)

$$= 0.3 \times 0.4 = 0.12$$

P(only rained on Tuesday) = P(no rain Monday) × P(rain Tuesday)

$$= 0.7 \times 0.4 = 0.28$$

It is more likely that it rained on Tuesday.

NAILIT!

Make sure you state on which day it is more likely to have rained. It is not up to the examiner to decide this from your working out.

You may not always be told to draw the tree diagram. You may also need to use algebra to work out the answer.

WORKIT!

A box contains cartons of orange juice and apple juice in the ratio 2 : 1.
Two cartons of juice are taken out of the box at random.
The probability that both cartons are apple juice is $\frac{7}{69}$.

How many cartons of apple juice are there in the box?

Let the number of apple juice cartons be x.

Use a variable for one part of the ratio.

$$P(2 \text{ apple}) = \frac{x}{3x} \times \frac{x-1}{3x-1} = \frac{7}{69}$$

$3x$ is total number of cartons using both parts of the ratio.

$$69x(x-1) = 7 \times 3x(3x-1)$$

$$23(x-1) = 7(3x-1)$$

Divide both sides by $3x$.

$$23x - 23 = 21x - 7$$

$$2x = 16$$

$$x = 8$$

Solve the equation for x.

There are 8 cartons of apple juice in the box.

Draw a tree diagram.

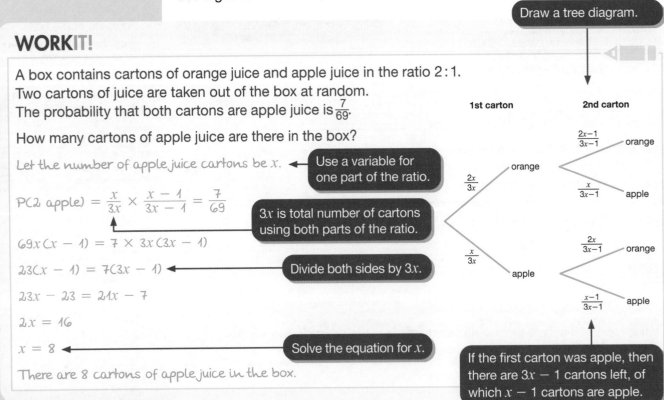

If the first carton was apple, then there are $3x - 1$ cartons left, of which $x - 1$ cartons are apple.

Frequency trees

The results of a probability experiment can be displayed using a **frequency tree**. The frequency tree can then be used to estimate the probability of certain scenarios.

WORKIT!

There are 350 staff working in an office. The ratio of males to females is 4:3.

For the male staff, the ratio of the number of full-time staff to the number of part-time staff is 3:1.

For the female staff the ratio of the number of part-time staff to the number of full-time staff is 2:1.

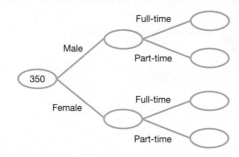

a   Complete the frequency tree.

Males : females = 4 : 3   7 parts = 350, so 1 part = 50

Number of males = 4 × 50 = 200

Number of females = 3 × 50 = 150

Males: full-time : part-time = 3 : 1   4 parts = 200, so 1 part = 50

Number of males full-time = 3 × 50 = 150

Number of males part-time = 1 × 50 = 50

Females: part-time : full-time = 2 : 1   3 parts = 150, so 1 part = 50

Number of females part-time = 2 × 50 = 100

Number of females full-time = 1 × 50 = 50

Fill in the frequency tree with the calculated values.

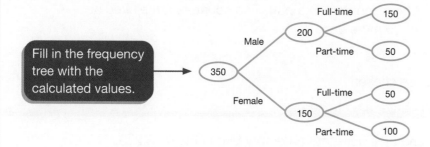

There are 150 female staff out of a total of 350 staff.

Out of 150 female staff, 50 of them work full-time.

b Using the frequency tree, work out the probability that a member of staff chosen at random is a female who works full-time.

Probability a female is chosen $= \frac{150}{350} = \frac{3}{7}$

Probability that the female works full-time $= \frac{50}{150} = \frac{1}{3}$

P(female who works full-time) $= \frac{3}{7} \times \frac{1}{3} = \frac{1}{7}$ ← Use the AND rule.

DOIT!

Write some revision cards containing all the main points and formulae for probability.

✓ CHECKIT!

1 There are 3 red and 7 blue counters in a bag. Two counters are picked at random, one at a time, from the bag.

Work out the probability that:

a two red counters are chosen

b a red and a blue counter are chosen.

2 Hannah puts green and blue balls into an empty bag in the ratio 2:3.

Zak takes at random two balls from the bag. The probability he takes two blue balls is $\frac{33}{95}$.

How many balls did Hannah put in the bag?

3 Saskia goes to the airport to catch a flight. The probability that there is a long queue to check in is 0.7. The probability that there is a long queue at security is 0.5.

a Copy and complete the tree diagram.

b Calculate the probability that there is a short queue at both check-in and security.

c Calculate the probability of a long queue at either check-in or security, or at both.

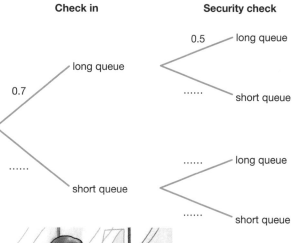

4 A secondary school has an upper school of 450 students and a lower school of 500 students. In the upper school, 60% of the students are male and in the lower school 55% are male.

a Copy and complete the frequency tree.

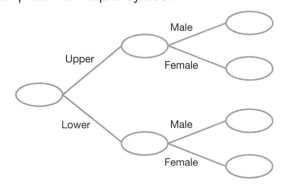

b A student is chosen at random from the school. Find the probability that the student is male.

Venn diagrams and probability

Venn diagrams can be used to work out probability.

The **universal set** is the whole collection of things, called **elements**, being considered. Usually an element is a number (e.g. {3, 5, 8} or an item {Jack, Queen, King}).

Sets are parts of the universal set and are shown as labelled circles/ovals on the Venn diagram. Sets contain some of the elements in the universal set and no other elements.

The universal set is labelled with the Greek letter ξ (ξ, pronounced ksi).

Curly brackets are used to show sets.

The Venn diagram shows the universal set ξ = {1, 2, 3, 4, 5, 6, 7, 8, 9, 10}, set A = {2, 3, 5, 6, 7, 8} and set B = {1, 2, 4, 6, 9}.

The number of elements in set A is referred to as n(A): in this example n(A) = 6.

SNAPIT! Venn diagrams

Here are the terms used for different areas on the Venn diagram:

Expression	Term	Meaning	Set of numbers
A ∩ B	A intersect B	All the elements in set A which are also in set B	{2, 6}
A ∪ B	A union B	All the elements in both set A and set B	{1, 2, 3, 4, 5, 6, 7, 8, 9}
A′	A complement	All the elements in the universal set that are not in set A	{1, 4, 9, 10}

WORKIT!

The Venn diagram shows all the factors of 36 and 40.

Set A is the set of all the factors of 36.

Set B is the set of all the factors of 40.

a Write down all the numbers in A ∩ B and describe their significance.

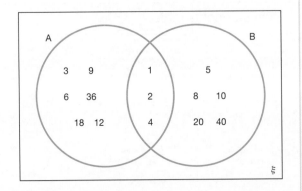

A ∩ B = {1, 2, 4}, all the numbers that are a factor of both 36 and 40

All the numbers in the intersection between A and B

b A number is picked at random from the set A ∪ B. Find the probability that it is an even number.

P(even number in A ∪ B) = $\frac{10}{14}$ = $\frac{5}{7}$ ◄——— A ∪ B is the set of all the numbers in A and B: 14 numbers of which 10 are even.

c A number is picked at random from the set B′.
Find the probability that the number is a multiple of 9.

B′ = {3, 6, 9, 12, 18, 36}

P(multiple of 9 in B′) = $\frac{3}{6}$ = $\frac{1}{2}$ ◄——— Three elements of B′ are multiples of 9.

WORKIT!

There are 43 members in a youth club.
25 play badminton, 16 play chess and 20 play tennis. 5 play all three games. 2 play chess and tennis but not badminton. 7 play tennis and badminton only. 6 members play only chess. 4 members do not play any games.

a Draw a Venn diagram showing the above information.

16 play chess, so number who play badminton and chess only
= 16 − (6 + 5 + 2) = 3

25 play badminton, so the number who play badminton only
= 25 − (3 + 5 + 7) = 10

20 play tennis, so the number who play tennis only = 20 − (7 + 5 + 2) = 6

First add all the easy information to the Venn diagram.

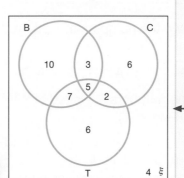

Put the values into the diagram as you work them out.

Use the information in the question to work out the other values for the Venn diagram.

b A member of the club is picked at random.
Find the probability that this member only plays badminton.

P(badminton only) = $\frac{10}{43}$

c Out of those members who play badminton, find the probability that they play only **one** other game.

P(badminton and only one other game)
= $\frac{7 + 3}{10 + 7 + 3 + 5}$ = $\frac{10}{25}$ = $\frac{2}{5}$

NAILIT!

Check that all the numbers on the Venn diagram add up to the total given in the question.

DO IT!

Produce pairs of cards containing a shaded area on a Venn diagram and the expression for the area (e.g. A ∩ B). Practise matching the cards.

CHECK IT!

1 The diagram below is a Venn diagram.

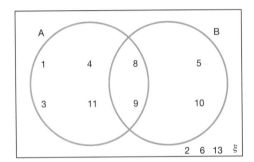

a Write down the numbers that are in the set:

   i A ∪ B   **ii** A ∩ B   **iii** A′

b One of the numbers is picked at random. Find P(B′).

2 In a sixth form of 180 students:
84 students take at least one science
40 study all three sciences
1 student studies only physics
12 study physics and biology only
48 study physics and chemistry
15 study biology and chemistry, but not physics
65 study chemistry.

a A student is chosen at random from those who take science. What is the probability that the student takes all three sciences?

b A student is chosen at random from those who take science. What is the probability that the student takes only one science?

c Out of those students studying physics, find the probability that they also study chemistry.

3 The universal set is the set of integers from 1 to 20. Set A is the set of square numbers. Set B is the set of all even numbers.

a Complete the following Venn diagram.

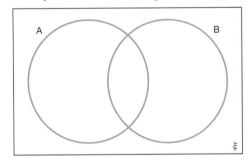

b An integer is chosen at random. Find the probability that it is not an even or square number.

1 A bag contains 4 red counters, 3 green counters and 3 white counters.

A counter is taken at random from the bag and not replaced. Then a second counter is taken from the bag.

a Complete the tree diagram.

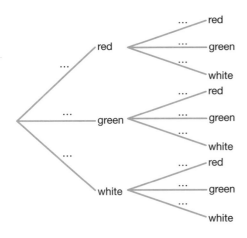

b Calculate the probability that the two counters taken from the bag are the same colour.

c Calculate the probability that the two counters taken from the bag are different colours.

2 A bag contains 3 red balls and x black balls.

Two balls are removed at random from the bag.

The probability that two black balls are chosen is $\frac{7}{15}$.

a Show that $4x^2 - 25x - 21 = 0$.

b Find the total number of balls in the bag.

c Find the probability of the two balls being different colours.

3 60 students were asked which sports they liked watching from football, tennis and motor racing.

All 60 students liked watching at least one sport.

10 students liked watching all three sports.

3 liked watching football and motor racing only.

15 liked watching tennis and motor racing.

29 liked watching motor racing.

18 liked watching football and tennis.

41 liked watching football.

a What is the probability that a student chosen at random from the group only liked to watch motor racing?

b A student is chosen from those who liked motor racing. What is the probability that the student also liked tennis?

4 In a certain country, out of 500 defendants being tried by the law courts 75% committed the crime. Of those who committed the crime, 80% were found guilty. Of those who did not commit the crime, 20% were found guilty.

a Complete the frequency tree to show this information.

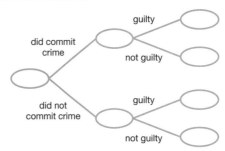

b A defendant was chosen at random from the 500 defendants. Find the probability that the defendant was found guilty.

c A defendant was chosen at random from those who did not commit the crime. Find the probability that the defendant was found guilty.

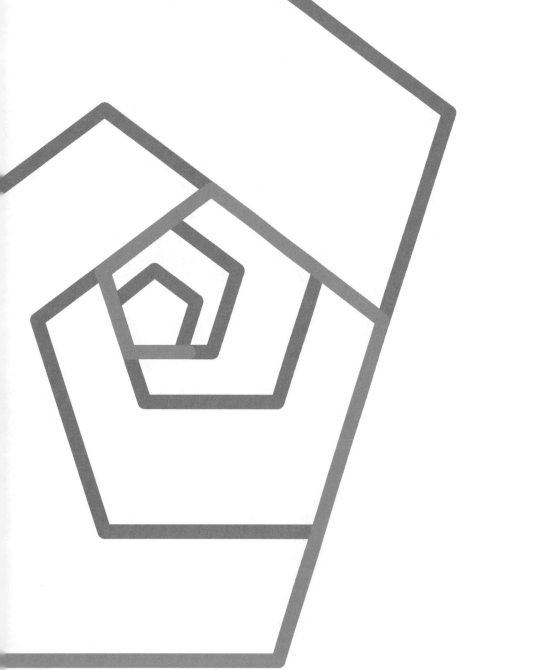

EXAM PRACTICE

Probability
The basics of probability

SNAPIT!

If all outcomes are equally likely

Probability = $\frac{\text{number of ways something can happen}}{\text{total number of possible outcomes}}$

This is a mathematical calculation and is known as **theoretical probability**.

① Two dice are thrown and the scores are added together. (★★)

The sample space diagram for the total score is shown below. The first row has been completed.

a Complete the sample space diagram. (2 marks)

Dice 1

	1	2	3	4	5	6
1	2	3	4	5	6	7
2						
3						
4						
5						
6						

Dice 2

b Find the probability of obtaining a score of 12. (1 mark)

....

c Find the probability of obtaining a score that is a prime number. (1 mark)

....

d What is the most likely score? Give a reason for your answer. (1 mark)

....

....

[Total: 5 marks]

② A box of chocolates contains three different types of chocolate.

The table shows the number of chocolates of each type.

	Truffle	Mint	Caramel
Number of chocolates	$2x + 1$	x	$2x$

You need to find the value of x first.

A chocolate is chosen at random. The probability of the chocolate being a mint is $\frac{4}{21}$. (★★★)

a Calculate the total number of chocolates in the box. (2 marks)

b Calculate the probability of choosing a truffle. (1 mark)

....

....

[Total: 3 marks]

③ Amy and Bethany each throw a fair dice.

Calculate the probability that the score on Amy's dice is (★★★★)

a equal to the score on Bethany's dice (2 marks)

....

b greater than the score on Bethany's dice (2 marks)

....

[Total: 4 marks]

Probability experiments

1. A pentagonal unbiased spinner with sides numbered 1 to 5 was spun 100 times. (★★★)

   The frequency that the spinner landed on each number was recorded in the table below.

Score on spinner	1	2	3	4	5
Frequency	18	23	22	19	18

   a   Abdul says that the spinner must be biased because if it was fair the frequency for each score would be the same. Explain why Abdul is wrong. (1 mark)

   ....

   ....

   b   Calculate the relative frequency of obtaining a score of 3 on the spinner. Give your answer as a fraction in its simplest form. (2 marks)

   ....

   c   If the spinner was spun 500 times, use the relative frequency to estimate how many times the spinner would give a score of 4. (1 mark)

   ....

   [Total: 4 marks]

2 A hexagonal spinner with sides numbered from 1 to 6 has the following relative frequencies of scores from 1 to 6. (★★★)

Score	1	2	3	4	5	6
Relative frequency	$3x$	0.05	$2x$	0.25	0.2	0.1

a Calculate the value of x. (2 marks)

....

b Calculate the relative frequency of obtaining a score of 1. (1 mark)

....

c The spinner was spun 80 times. Estimate how many times the score was 5. (1 mark)

....

[Total: 4 marks]

 **STRETCH**IT!

Playing cards are interesting because they offer a lot of different probabilities. If you draw a card, it could be: red, black, a heart, a diamond, a club, a spade, an ace, a picture card, a 5 and so on. Think about how these different probabilities affect the games people play – and conjuring tricks too.

The AND and OR rules

SNAPIT!

The OR rule: Probability of A or B happening: P(A OR B) = P(A) + P(B)

The AND rule: Probability of A and B happening: P(A AND B) = P(A) × P(B)

① A card is chosen at random from a pack of 52 playing cards and noted. The card is returned, the pack shuffled and a second card chosen. (★★★)

Find the probability the two cards were

a two picture cards (1 mark)

c the queen of diamonds and the queen of hearts. (1 mark)

....

....

b an ace and a picture card (1 mark)

....

[Total: 3 marks]

② A bag contains 10 marbles: 3 red, 5 blue and 2 green.

A marble is removed from the bag and its colour noted before it is put back into the bag.

Another marble is removed and its colour is also noted. (★★★★)

a Explain what is meant by independent events. (1 mark)

....

b Calculate the probability that two red marbles were picked. (2 marks)

c Calculate the probability that the two marbles were red and blue. (3 marks)

....

....

[Total: 6 marks]

③ The probability that Aisha is given maths homework on a certain day is $\frac{3}{5}$. The probability she is given French homework is $\frac{3}{7}$. The probability she is given geography homework is $\frac{1}{4}$. (★★★★)

a Work out the probability that she is given homework in all three subjects.

(2 marks)

b Work out the probability that she is not given homework in any of these subjects.

(2 marks)

....

....

[Total: 4 marks]

Tree diagrams

WORKIT!

A box contains 7 counters: 3 red and 4 blue.

A counter taken at random from the box is red.

A second counter is taken at random.

What is the probability that the second counter is red if

a the first counter was put back in the box

Number of red counters in box = 3

Total number of counters = 7

P(red) = $\frac{3}{7}$

b the first counter was not put back in the box?

Number of red counters in box = 2

Total number of counters = 6

P(red) = $\frac{2}{6} = \frac{1}{3}$

(1) From a group of children consisting of 4 girls and 6 boys, 2 children are picked at random to take part in an interview.

Work out the probability that (★★★★)

a two girls are chosen (3 marks)

....

b a boy and a girl are chosen. (3 marks)

....

[Total: 6 marks]

2 There are 450 pupils in a junior school, 56% of whom are boys.

The ratio of boys who have school dinners to the boys who have a packed lunch is 2:1. The ratio of girls who have school dinners to the girls who have a packed lunch is 5:4 (★★★★)

> Make sure you understand the difference between probability trees and frequency trees.

a Complete the frequency tree. (4 marks)

b Using the frequency tree, work out the probability that a pupil chosen at random from the school is a girl who has a school dinner. (2 marks)

....

c Using the frequency tree, work out the probability that a pupil chosen at random from the school has a school dinner. (2 marks)

> There are two ways in which this can happen so you need to find the probability for each and then add them together.

....

[Total: 8 marks]

3 A bag contains 9 marbles, of which 5 are red, 3 are green and 1 is yellow. Three marbles are chosen at random from the bag.

Giving your answer correct to 3 decimal places, calculate the probability of choosing (★★★★★)

a 1 marble of each colour (3 marks)

> Draw a probability tree to help you.

....

b no green marbles (2 marks)

....

c 3 marbles of the same colour. (3 marks)

....

[Total: 8 marks]

Venn diagrams and probability

(1) The Venn diagram shows the universal set with two subsets A and B. (★★★)

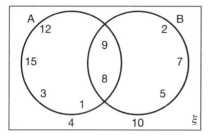

Write down the numbers in

a A ∩ B (1 mark)

....

b A ∪ B (1 mark)

....

c B′ (1 mark)

....

d (A ∪ B)′ (1 mark)

....

[Total: 4 marks]

(2) ξ = {1, 2, 3, 4, 5, 6, 7, 8, 9, 10, 11, 12, 13, 14, 15}

P = prime numbers

O = odd numbers (★★★★)

a Complete the Venn diagram. (3 marks)

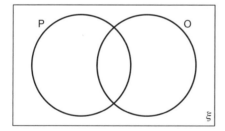

b One of the numbers in the universal set is chosen at random.

Calculate the probability that the number chosen is in P ∩ O. (2 marks)

.... **[Total: 5 marks]**

(3) A survey asked 100 sports students about the types of sport they played: individual, small team, large team. It found that 6 students played individual, small team and large team sports; 15 only played individual sports; 10 played both individual and small team sports; and 18 played both small team and large team sports. Overall, there were 41 who played individual sports and 30 who played small team sports. (★★★★★)

a A sports student is chosen at random. What is the probability that the student plays team sports? (4 marks)

b A student is chosen at random from those students who play large team sports. What is the probability that they also play small team sports? (2 marks)

.... **[Total: 6 marks]**

Answers

Revision answers

The basics of probability p.8

1 $\frac{8}{125}$

2 a 0

  b $\frac{1}{5}$

  c $\frac{11}{20}$

Probability experiments p.10

1 a 0.21 (to 2 d.p.)

  b 0.14 (to 2 d.p.)

  c Sean is wrong. 120 spins is a small number of spins and it is only over a very large number of spins that the relative frequencies may start to be nearly the same.

2 a 0.04   **b** 600 cans

3 45 apples

The AND and OR rules p.12

1 a Independent events are events where the probability of one event does not influence the probability of another event occurring. Here it means that the probability of the first set of traffic lights being red does not affect the probability of the second set being red.

  b 0.06   **c** 0.56

2 a $\frac{7}{48}$ **b** $\frac{1}{32}$

Tree diagrams p.16

1 a $\frac{1}{15}$

  b $\frac{7}{15}$

2 20 balls

3 a

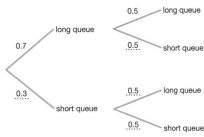

  b 0.15

  c 0.85

4 a

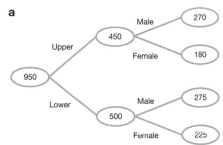

---

b $\frac{109}{190}$ or 0.57

Venn diagrams and probability p.20

1 a i {1, 3, 4, 5 8, 9, 10, 11}

    ii {8, 9}

    iii {2, 5, 6. 10, 13}

  b $\frac{7}{11}$

2

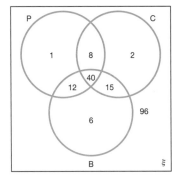

  a $\frac{10}{21}$

  b $\frac{3}{28}$

  c $\frac{48}{61}$

3 a

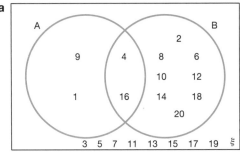

  b $P = \frac{8}{20} = \frac{2}{5}$

Review it! p.21

1 a

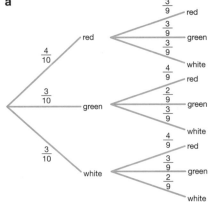

  b $\frac{4}{15}$

  c $\frac{11}{15}$

2 a

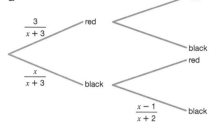

$$P(\text{two black}) = \left(\frac{x}{x+3}\right) \times \left(\frac{x-1}{x+2}\right) = \frac{7}{15}$$

$$15x(x-1) = 7(x+3)(x+2)$$
$$15x^2 - 15x = 7x^2 + 35x + 42$$
$$8x^2 - 50x - 42 = 0$$
$$4x^2 - 25x - 21 = 0$$

b 10 balls

c $\frac{7}{15}$

3

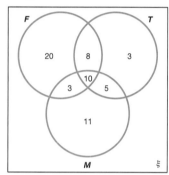

a $\frac{11}{60}$ **b** $\frac{15}{29}$

4 a

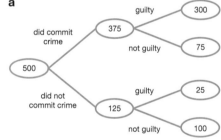

b $\frac{13}{20}$ **c** $\frac{1}{5}$

Exam practice answers

The basics of probability p.23

1 a

		1	**2**	**3**	**4**	**5**	**6**
	1	2	3	4	5	6	7
	2	3	4	5	6	7	8
Dice 2	**3**	4	5	6	7	8	9
	4	5	6	7	8	9	10
	5	6	7	8	9	10	11
	6	7	8	9	10	11	12

Dice 1

b $\frac{1}{36}$ **c** $\frac{5}{12}$

d 7 The number of ways of scoring 7 is 6 out of 36 outcomes, which is more than any other score.

2 a 21 chocolates   **b** $\frac{3}{7}$

3

Bethany

		1	**2**	**3**	**4**	**5**	**6**
	1	1, 1	1, 2	1, 3	1, 4	1, 5	1, 6
	2	2, 1	2, 2	2, 3	2, 4	2, 5	2, 6
	3	3, 1	3, 2	3, 3	3, 4	3, 5	3, 6
Amy	**4**	4, 1	4, 2	4, 3	4, 4	4, 5	4, 6
	5	5, 1	5, 2	5, 3	5, 4	5, 5	5, 6
	6	6, 1	6, 2	6, 3	6, 4	6, 5	6, 6

a $\frac{1}{6}$ **b** $\frac{5}{12}$

Probability experiments p.24

1 a He is wrong because 100 spins is a very small number of trials. To approach the theoretical probability you would have to spin many more times. Only when the number of spins is extremely large will the frequencies start to become similar.

b $\frac{11}{50}$ **c** 95

2 a $x = 0.08$ **b** 0.24   **c** 16

The AND and OR rules p.26

1 a $\frac{9}{169}$ **b** $\frac{3}{169}$ **c** $\frac{1}{52} \times \frac{1}{52} = \frac{1}{2704}$

2 a When an event has no effect on another event, they are said to be independent events. Here the colour of the first marble has no effect on the colour of the second marble.

b $\frac{9}{100}$ **c** $\frac{3}{10}$

3 a $\frac{9}{140}$ **b** $\frac{6}{35}$

Tree diagrams p.27

1 a $\frac{2}{15}$ **b** $\frac{8}{15}$

2 a

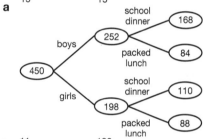

b $\frac{11}{45}$ **c** $\frac{139}{225}$

3 a 0.179 (to 3 d.p.)   **b** 0.238 (to 3 d.p.)
   c 0.131 (to 3 d.p.)

Venn diagrams and probability p.29

1 a 9, 8   **c** 1, 3, 4, 10, 12, 15
   b 1, 2, 3, 5, 7, 8, 9, 12, 15   **d** 4, 10

2 a

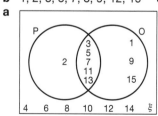

b $\frac{1}{3}$

3 a $\frac{17}{20}$ **b** $\frac{18}{73}$

SCHOLASTIC

GCSE Skills

Build confidence with targeted skills practice

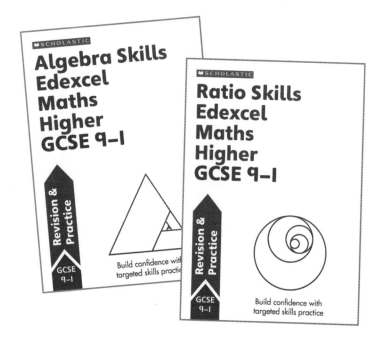

Revise GCSE Maths topics in greater depth

- Clear and focused explanations of tricky topics

- Questions that offer additional challenge

- Deepen understanding and apply knowledge

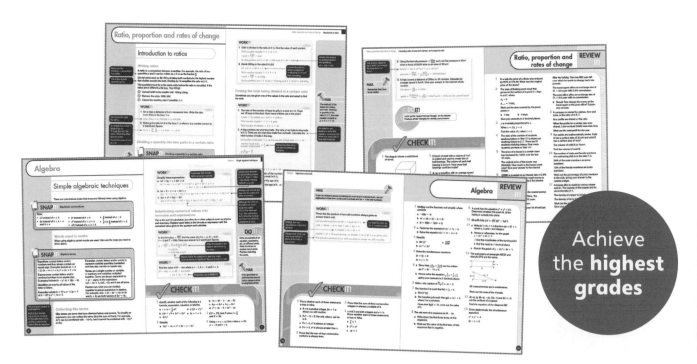

Achieve the **highest grades**

Revision & Practice ▸ **10-Minute Tests** ▸ **National Tests** ▸ **Catch-up & Challenge**

Find out more at **www.scholastic.co.uk/learn-at-home**